HOWL TOO, EH?
and other satires

by
ENDRE FARKAS
&
KEN NORRIS

with special guest appearances
by

ARTIE GOLD
&
TOM KONYVES

NUAGE
EDITIONS

Book design & typesetting by Karen Haughian.

Dépôt légal, Bibliothéque nationale du Québec and the National Library of Canada.

NuAge Editions
P.O. Box 8, Station E,
Montreal, QC, H2T 3A5

Contents

Satire: the art of
giving a good laugh,
getting the sharp edge of the pen
to cut to the heart of the matter.
Get the point?
Sit on it!

Dedication

To — Allen Ginsberg, a blessed beat who made this possible and whose howl is still howling.

— The Véhicule Poets, who were, are and are to come.

— The real poets of Canada and the world who dance, chant, sing, laugh, tape videos, write and care; who go crazy when they see poems pinned like butterflies to the page by undertakers; who plan jailbreaks for poems imprisoned by sensitive moo-eyed melancholics, who are messy in the holiest sense because their doors and hearts are open to those who care.

— The future. May our poems unscrew the locks from the doors! Unscrew the solitudes!

Introduction

These poems are a result of living now,
a result of living in a country that knows itself
by what it is not,
written while waiting for the English and French elite
to decide to merge or separate their assets.

These poems are a collaboration between immigrants,
fifth columnists who know that they live
in an immigrant world
"Oh Immigrant"
Doesn't sound too bad, eh?

These poems are about our age here and now,
about interesting living, about being human.
Even in Canada, we hold these poems to be
self-evident, eternal.

And of form this must be said:
A borrower and a lender be.
We borrowed with the most honourable intentions.
Actually, we call it Free Trade.
Poets have been engaged in it for centuries,
but our Free Trade exploits no one.
Thank you Mr Ginsberg,
Thank you Mr Eliot,
Thank you Mr Cohen,
and everyone else.

When we were younger and the world was younger, we hung out in unheated second-floor art spaces, in all-night restaurants for hookers and the homeless, and in each other's kitchens and bedrooms. We ranted, we raved, we read, we made plans and love. We ran poetry readings, created performances, mimeowed *Mouse Eggs,* and started publishing books. We collaborated.

Collaboration was an essential element in our individual as well as our collective lives in the seventies. We were just starting to write and found courage through each other's encouragement. It wasn't uncritical, but it was supportive. This support plus our hanging out in alternative (collective) art galleries where we saw visual artists working together, exploring new art forms, like performance art, made some of us want to do it too. We began individually by making poems that were meant to be performed rather than read out loud, poems for more than one voice, texts for poets and dancers and video poetry. Collaborative writing was a natural development in this kind of environment.

It wasn't a concious decision, but a by-product of our hanging out. It happened sitting around a table in a brasserie and passing a sheet around and each writing phrases, not knowing what the others had written. It evolved to agreeing to write on a topic, i.e. 8 1/2 x 11 which was also to be the size, to six of us sending a text through the mail and adding, deleting, collaging, until we came up with "Drummer Boy Raga."

As we got older and the world got much older, we went our separate ways into our grown-up lives. But we still had the collaborative spirit. That is why, and how, this book evolved. Ken and I wrote "Howl Too, Eh?" in 1986. We found the form that was perfect for this subject (a perfect marriage of form and content) and then ping-ponged phrases back and forth across his Duluth Street kitchen table. People would come, listen in, throw in an idea, an image, some trivia, and go.

"Maple Leaf Rag," "Au Canada," "The Only Tourist in Bangor, Maine Turns His Thoughts Home-ward" and "Language Cops" are more recent, and even though they have only one of our names attached to them, they too are collaborations. One of us would have the idea and sweat it out, and then mail it or phone it to the other who would delete and add and send it back. And so it went till one yelled "uncle." Usually the one who had started the piece had the last word.

I don't know who thought of it first, but one of us did suggest that we include a couple of the other Véhicule poets. Tom was a natural because Ken had worked with him on a couple of pieces and a few sections of "See-Saw" seemed right.

Artie was the next obvious choice, because he was always disassociating. He was the disassociate editor at Véhicule Press, he was the disassociate participant in *A Real Good Goosin* (a round table debate with Louis Dudek by mail), and the disassociate editor of *The Véhicule Poets* anthology. He also has a wicked sense of humour and "The Pumpkin Eaters" fit the tone of this book.

A sense of humour is one of the elements in the work of the Véhicule Poets. We knew that humour is one of the essential and unique qualities that make us human. And we knew/know that it is one of the most effective ways to attack the injustice, hypocrisy, stupidity and evil that also seem to be unique to human beings. Satire is the child who points an embarassing finger and shouts loudly, "Look, the emperor has no clothes."

Our intent in *Howl Too, Eh?* was to write poems that struck the funny bone .

Howl Too, Eh?

I see the best dressed minds of my g-g-generation,
 trendy, coked to the nose, hooked on Trivial
 Pursuit,
driving their free spirited BMWs through ghetto
 streets looking for the ideal cockroached flats to
 fix and flip,
Young Upwardly Mobile Urban Professionals
 yearning for the neo-nouvelle connection to the
 bottom lines of 2nd Début encounters with the
 Third Wave of café-au-lait-coloured mid-life
 Passages.

The Fifties

Who, Spocked, Seussed, and Pablumed, boomed
 after the Second Boom Boom into the land of
 suburban split-level nurseries,
who were nursed on germ-free Lysol nipples and
 toilet trained by Captain Kangaroo,
who were Howdy Doodyed by Clarabell & Princess
 Summerfall Winterspring on plastic-covered
 couches while in the dens Father Knew Best
 with Donna Reed,

who always came home with Lassie, Lassie II,
Timmy, Timmy II, and their puppies,
who hopped along Happy Trails with Roy, Dale,
Bullet and an unstuffed Trigger,
who were Kemo Sabeed by the Masked Man,
who fought savage redskins with long knives,
thunder-sticks, forked tongues, and Rusty
Rin Tin Tins,
who sent in box tops for parents like Ozzie & Harriet,
who were snapped, crackled, and popped for
breakfast, Wonder Breaded for lunch, and
TV dinnered for supper,
who wanted Spring Byington and Walter Brennan for
grandparents but had to settle for old-country
Bubbes and Zaides,
who saw Dick and Jane see Mom and Dad see Spot
poop on Sally,
who left it to Beaver,
who passed air raid drills under desks with friendly
phys-ed teachers who preached the godlessness
of Dirty Commie Ruskies and the importance of
white socks and cold showers,
who, wearing towels and sisters' panties, leaped
from chrome and arborite tabletops into
Clearasiled puberty,
who, after watching Annette Funicello in Mouse ears,
jerked off into their Mickey Mouse pajamas,

12

who sneaked into girls' washrooms to be aroused
    but were mystified by the Kotex vending
    machines instead,
who bought Romance Comics for their philosophy,
    morality, and Frederick's of Hollywood ads,
who, wearing high heels for the first time, tripped
    descending Loretta Young's staircase,
who wanted Kookie's comb, Anka's shoulder, and
    Elvis' hips,
who, with soldered beehive hairdos, in itchy pink
    mohairs over bras stuffed with Kleenex and
    crinolined skirts over invincible girdles,
    went to the sock-hop with crewcuts,
    Brylcreemed to their "little dab'll do yas,"
    faces burnt by that something in the Aqua Velva,
    and Lavoris-scrubbed breaths for the after
    at the lookout,
who danced chinos to taffetta to the crotch-music of
    Elvis clones,
who, at the lookout after the hop, went so far
    but not past their reputations and wouldn't
    French or touch *it* because it was *icky*,
who begged for it and promised respect after and
    forever,
who, one Sunday night, watched "A REALLY BIG
    SHOE" starring Topo Gigio and John, Paul,
    George, and Ringo, let down their hair and were
    never the same.
    Yeah! Yeah! Yeah!

The Sixties

Who knew that something was happening and so
    smoked hemp rope and baked banana peels.
    Mellow Yellow!
who felt nothing, not even a buzz, as they
    contemplated the lint in their navels and the
    cosmic significance of the cracks in the plaster.
    Deep, Man! Deep!
who gargled with Electric Kool-Aid and flossed with
    seaweed to greet the Age of Aquarius.
    Hair, Baby!
who breakfasted on near-risen bread, Alice B. Toklas
    cookies, and turnip tea.
    Bliss Me Out!
who bleached and patched their bell-bottoms,
    tie-dyed everything in sight, and grew weed and
    hair in and on anything that was organic.
    Meatball!
who turned on, tuned in, and dropped into the lotus
    position to watch the Greening of Amerika in the
    horizontal patterns of colour TVs.
    Medium Cool, Man!
who fringed their vests, joined the tribe, massaged
    the message, moved into the basements of the
    global village, and took trippy trips on the
    spaced-out ship Earth!
    Far Out!

who heard it through the boycotted lettuce, pickles,
    onions, mustard, ketchup, relish, and grapevine.
    Right Off!
who boogied in the strobe lights of the Fillmore East
    and West at the same time.
    Like, Oh Wow!
who, granny glassed, Fu Manchued, love beaded,
    sandalwooded, and hash oiled, lay zapped on
    mattressed floors in Day-Glo rooms lit by black
    lights and listened to The Doors through the walls.
    Dy...na...mite!
who dropped out for a semester, graduated to the bed
    of Mrs Robinson, hitchhiked down Highway 61
    to a commune to commune in cosmic group sex in
    fields where black flies bit alternative asses.
    Bummer!
who went macrobiotic, eating tofu burgers at Veggie
    Kings, drinking chicory cola at the Karma Kafé,
    and night after night experienced oneness with
    alfalfa sprouts, garbanzo beans, milkweed soup,
    smashed millet, 20-grain bread, and endless
    blissed brown rice.
    Yin Yang!
who named their homebirthed children Apricot,
    Melody, Harmony, Radish, Avocado, Frodo,
    Compost, Solar Power, Moon Unit, and God.
    Groovy!

who formed New Age daycares which emphasized
candle making, sun dialing, metric numerology,
astrology, dowsing and dealing.
Summerhill!

who lost their virginity at least twice at be-ins and
found their innocence at sit-ins for free speech,
free love and free toilets.
Peace & Love!

who, returning from Tijuana in their VW vans, got
busted for a litre of patchouli oil.
What A Drag, Man!

who sang "You can get anything you want at Alice's
Restaurant" in two-part harmony by himself,
wearing a dress, and still got drafted.
Ho Chi Minh!

who enlisted in the Peace Corps and volunteered to
work in Tangiers on the Marrakesh Express.
Good Shit!

who didn't need a Weatherman to know which way
the wind blew in Canada.
Far Fucking Cold!

who, by burning their bras, freed their breasts, raised
our consciousness, liberated personkind, and
titillated pigs.
Ms!

who, California Dreaming, vibrated Big Sur, beaded
Haight-Ashbury, and flew to Woodstock in their
paisley flower-powered astral planes.
Keep On Truckin'!

who threw the I Ching to learn of the *Difficulty at the
   Beginning* of mastering the Frisbee.
   Good Vibrations!
who, in Mao caps, Che Guevara beards, and
   macramé pants, studied t'ai chi, do in, kung fu,
   and stretch mark charts under the guidance of
   Ra Bi Bum Krep La.
   Ommmmmmm!
who, like dig it, like it's cool, man, like WOW!, like
   Dynamite!, like I mean the yin and the yang of it
   felt so groovy in the twelfth chakra; like I mean
   it's like far fucking out; like I mean, had a new
   explanation.
   Like Yeah!
who shaved their heads and dabbed on enlightened
   pigeon shit and chanted for Krishna, the
   Maharishi, the Mahariji, the Montreal Canadiens
   and the Consciousness of Cash.
   Hare! Hare!
who found the meaning of the universe in Zen & the
   Art of New Age Enterprising and opened up a
   chain of boutiques specializing in used mantras.
   Siddhartha!
who went rolfing for the weekend and never came
   back, leaving behind water pipes, Sgt. Pepper
   uniforms, and scratched copies of *Magical Mystery
   Tour*, and actualised in singles bars wearing
   coke spoons on gold chains and dancing to the
   sound of the Village People.
   Woo! Woo!

The Seventies

Who smoked extra-long, extra-thin, extra-mild
    cigarettes, cigarettes, cigarettes and between
    sincere drags asked, "What's your sign? what's
    your sign? what's your sign?"
who cruised discos looking for the Unisex connection
    and anyone to go home with and went and left
    no meaningful phone numbers behind,
who encountered in sport boutiques, searching for
    their primal matching head and wrist bands; in
    tanning tanks, absorbing the rays of instant
    sensitivity; in exclusive racquet clubs, releasing
    deeply felt sweat; and in lean cuisines, making
    meaningful contact with cottage cheese,
who jogged through the invisible Wall, seeking the
    visionary running shoe,
who revealed their honesty by opening their hearts
    and shirts to the navel,
who devoured *The Joy of Sexual Celibacy,*
    I'm OK, You're So-So, and
    How to be Your Only Best Friend,
who breakfasted on designer croissants, Art Nouveau
    orange juice, and personally blended,
    decaffeinated cappuccinos,
who took meetings on water beds filled with Perrier,
who came out of tacky closets and stepped into divine
    steam baths,

who found their love in tennis,
who had their philosophy shaped by Vidal Sassoon,
who, because the cosmos vibrated on the beaches of
    Club Med, went and returned with the absolute
    tan and the fear of sexual diseases, and decided to
    get married and serious about their careers.

The Eighties

What icon of paper and gold opened our eyes and
captured our imagination?
MONEY!
Aesthetically decoupaged, *Decormagged*, and smartly
dressed at the trendiest laundromat.
MONEY!
Colour coordinated.
MONEY!
The crushed-velvet safe of happiness.
MONEY!
Whose fronts are sandblasted.
MONEY!
Whose presence is custom-designed.
MONEY!
Whose mind is pure cocaine!
MONEY!
Whose blood is Pernod.
MONEY!
Whose breasts are fashionably lifted
and separated.

MONEY!
Whose ears are tastefully pierced in at least
four places per lobe.
MONEY!
Whose vice is Miami.
MONEY!
Whose boutiques move from trendy
to trendier
to trendiest locale overnight.
MONEY!
Whose lover is a merging relationship.
MONEY!
Whose soul is golf.
MONEY!
Whose absence is managed by
Shame, Shamer & Shamest Inc.
MONEY!
Whose name is MINE!

MINE!
Multiple monogrammed bank accounts.
MINE!
Bill Blass-designed portfolios.
MINE!
Lakefront tax shelters.

Jimi Hendrix: We're with you in spirit
    every time we have an acid flashback
    in aerobics class
    every time we're at Republican rallies and
    hear "The Star-Spangled Banner"
    every time we are in the bedrooms and board
    rooms answering the question
    "Are you experienced?"
    every time we walk along Wall Street hoping
    that there is some kind of way into here.

Jim Morrison: We're with you in spirit
    every time we're in the Bay declaring
    "We want the world and we want it charged"
    every time we're in our condos, in our
    nouvelle cuisines, stalking the white asparagus,
    and are about to light our Jenn-Air fires
    every time we're in hot tubs with strange
    L.A. women interfacing our software
    every time we take our gecko lizards
    for a soft parade
    every time we put on English Leather.

Janis Joplin: We're with you in spirit
      every time you come over the radio
      of our Mercedes Benz
      every time we're in our offices where freedom is
      just another contract we can't afford to lose
      every time we put aside our lover's designer
      ball and chain and try a new deodorant
      every time we're in divorce courts where
      the lawyers take another piece of our portfolio,
      baby.

John Lennon: We're with you in spirit
      every time we imagine our penthouse
      above heaven
      every time we know that everyone's got
      something to hide except me
      and my accountant
      every time we're at the Exchange and see that the
      Board show our stocks bullish... "Oh Boy"
      every time we're at a terraced café with Michelle
      who's middle management at Ma Bell, and
      Lucy who wants real diamonds and
      who are always saying "Give sushi a chance"
      every time, after a hard day's night of freebasing,
      we put on our Walkmans, recline on our futons
      and listen to *Rubber Soul*.

Yuppie! Yuppie! Yuppie! Yuppie! Yuppie!
The salt & pepper pony tail is Yuppie!
The Oil of Oyvay is Yuppie!
The collapsed nose is Yuppie!
The discerning palate is Yuppie!
The tennis elbow is Yuppie!
The shin splint is Yuppie!
The White Swan soft ass is Yuppie!

Quality time spent stripping furniture is Yuppie!
Quality time spent assembling state of the art
CD videos is Yuppie!
Quality time spent at New Age lectures is Yuppie!
Quality time spent word processing is Yuppie!
Quality time spent buying quality is Yuppie!
Quality time is Yuppie!

Yuppie Eldridge Cleaver!
Yuppie Jerry Rubin!
Yuppie Jane Fonda!
Yuppie Hippies!
Yuppie Baby Boomers!
Yuppie us!

Yuppie God who art in a Ralph Lauren shirt
well-known may your products be.
Lead us into temptations
and deliver us from hard times and bad taste.
Forever and ever
Yuppie!

Maple Leaf Rag

I walked across the polluted St Lawrence and sat
under the rusted shadow of an abandoned VIA
locomotive to look at my country through
constitutional committeed-out eyes
and wondered why.

Brian Mulroney sat beside me
on his conservative behind.
Countryman, we thought very different thoughts;
me of Canada Canadian from sea to sea to CBC,
you of a Canada franchised from sea to sea
to oil-spilled sea.

The oily water mirrored the for-sale sky, in which the
for-sale sun crossed the for-sale Prairies, and sank
behind the for-sale Rockies.

Look at the maple leaves, I said
(no not the hockey team).
There was only a shadow against the sky,
pock-marked like Sudbury,
smelly from a dead branch plant.

I rushed up—horrified
it was my first acid maple leaf,
it evoked visions of a Canada past:

savages like Lief the Lucky,
other Europeans like Cabot and Cartier,
looking for La Chine and Indy
and Brébeuf and his brethren
fishing for redskin souls
coureur de bois chasing beavers in the woods,
hewers of wood, drawers of water,
planting their seeds,
Susanna roughing it in the bush,
Laura and her cow cross-border spying,
Fathers of Con-federation sugaring off,
and like Nature of Things,
when suddenly I had another vision
on television: images of our politicians
meeting at Meech Lake; custom-tailored men
dressed as real estate agents
selling our century 21.

And the gray maple leaf flag against the foreign sky
fluttered obediently over a castrated beaver.
And waiters sang
"When Irish eyes are smiling"
As they carved up the country
Like a sugar pie
For the voracious multinational mouths
My maple leaf! O little beaver!
I dropped my guard!

Je me souviens
that once upon a time
the land was the natives'
that is, no one's,
...but not for long.

This new Jerusalem,
these quelques arpents de neiges,
this country that God gave to Cain,
this obstacle on the way to the Orient,
this accident, has always been for sale.
And the bottom lines and pin-striped eyes
filled with U.S. envy are again calling for tenders.

I see The Chin That Walks Like A Man
and his patronaged senators deal this land
from the U.I.C. of Bonavista to the Arctic sea spills,
from the clear-cut forests to the Great Lake sewers, and
sing that this land was made for U.S.A.
And they are right!
I want in on the deal!

So I grabbed up the eviscerated maple leaf
and held it like an offering
and stood on guard with Big Chin
and declared to all: Yes!
We are dead, bleak, dusty, imageless Canadians,
we are hyphenated,
we are failed Americans,
we are for sale, reduced to clear.

We are blessed with an identity, I think.
We are all beautiful, brilliant maples
grown from seed
into sturdy maples
ready to be cut and shipped
from the glorious Group of Seven landscape.
to the homes of the brave and tarriff-free!

The Pumpkin Eaters

Oh Canada... Let me count the ways!
he's the new King of Israel (what a movie!
can't think what I might ask him
except perhaps if the "o" of "of" is to be capitalized.
When you beat me up oh Canada...
A last desperate attempt to sell me beer
over the television. wait. let me get my glasses.
why it's gone now! why did you make me
go through all this rigomarole for later of fuck-all?
Deep are your ways, Oh Canada,

                              long are your days
and you deign to let me sit on your lap!
Dazzling. dazzling. I swear by parliament
Your come is my immediate heartburn, birch
Your incisors bite my back like all the
beavers born and died since 1534.

"Oak-Canada"? no— wouldn't be the same: Oh
Canada ... keep it simple (painful) always maple!
Oh Canada, when you beat me up in your alleys,
I go black & blue on you, become gradually —
The Archbishop of Canadian Surrealism

                             (—Oh Canada ...)
what a movie! Even New Brunswick
has its finger up my ass!

A Hypermarché in Québec

I am in the hypermarché
        surveying
The prospects of the dairy section
When a female hand
        darts out
Of nowhere
And quickly plucks
        a huge round of Gouda cheese
From the shelf.
I am astounded—
        the cheese is beyond my means.
I turn to observe
        the face of the fortunate lady
Who can afford such extravagance.
She is a pigtailed beauty
Wrapped in a leather coat.
My emotions rise:
I love her and her cheese.

Quickly she is off, pushing
Her cart before I can say a word.
So I go on shopping.
I cool my passion by perusing
A section of frozen foods.
But later, over turnips, we meet again.
My love grows
Among the fruits and vegetables.

I decide to hold an asparagus
                    between my teeth
And dance with the flash of a flamenco;
But she disappears again
After taking advice from a counterman
About raisins.

I go back to my purchasing.
I squeeze a tomato, caress an eggplant,
Get excited about the price of lettuce.
In the bread section I decide
That if we ever meet again
                    I will give her a potato
To show her my affection.
If she accepts it
                    we will stroll through the store,
Our purchases in one mutual cart,
                    and sing the praises
Of The Hypermarché,
                    our divine matchmaker.
We will be like apple pie and ice cream,
                    pork and beans,
Baked potato and sour cream.
And I came here looking for food!
Bah, mere sustenance!
In this atmosphere of plenty
I have found love!

I remember that she has vanished among the aisles.
I look for her in the soups, cereals, salad dressings;
She is not there.
On to meats, cookies spices;
                    Alas!

In despair
I decide to check out;
She stands before me,
Emptying her cart out onto the conveyor.
She moves with such grace.
I observe the bounty of her cart.

She has cans of cat food,
A sure sign of loneliness.
Besides the cheese
                    which brought her
Into my blood
She has minor items.
She has an eggplant wrapped in cellophane.
My cart contains one too:
A common affinity.
A jar of meat sauce, stewed tomatoes.
She plays with a pigtail as she waits.
The check-out girl is slow.
My love speaks to the girl
in the language of the land;

Perhaps they briefly discuss Québec appetites.
I cannot tell; I am not a delicate crêpe
Nor a stocky bouillabaise; I am an English stew,
Worse than that, American,
A hamburger with french fries and a coke.

My heart sinks.
Her total is soon added,
The items placed in bags.
She pays and turns to leave.
I want to call out to her a recipe,
A helpful hint about spaghetti, anything.

Too late, too late.
All the way home
I long for her company at dinner.

Tom Konyves on *See/Saw*

In "See/Saw," I came closest to making an overt political statement—an unusual thing, really, considering English poetry in Québec. It began as "a poem for two voices, violin, dancer on bicycle, saws." "See/Saw" was my first experience in "writing" video. The collaboration resembled the Raga—I wrote the poem, then Ken Norris wrote between the lines.

The verbal level of Scene I spews forth venom generously, Ken's interruptions supportive and complementary to the poetic diatribe. Visually, the dialogue is interrupted by two loggers hard at work sawing a log in two—"I saw my country in half."

Scene III was adapted from a poem I had written, Anglophobia/Francophobia. Herein is reflected the frustration of English Quebecers at the time of the introduction of the language law: the absurd argument for "schooling." Out of loss of meaning we glean a list, a "pataphysical" list, ending with "boxing games."

The overt political theme of "See/Saw" still amazes me. I look at everything I have ever written, and I can't find a similar work. It was a unique moment in my life, attempt to fuse art and life to "say something." I was very serious about the concerns of "See/Saw," yet after each line was written, I was astonished to find the profusion of comic elements (ERA became earned run averages). The cynical led to the absurd. Thus, to a certain extent, "See/Saw" is theatre-video of the absurd.

From *See/Saw*, a poetic dialogue

I

Justice of the Piece:
I saw my country in half—broken-hearted, broken-
hearted, marching toward the grave beginnings of an
Earned Run Average, chock-full with servitude,
injustice & desertion.

First Mate:
Abominable...

Justice of the Piece:
I saw my country male and female. English, French.

First Mate:
Master and slave.

Justice of the Piece:
I saw my country male and female, approach the
future divorce-minded, face the firing squad of
poverty with fear. I saw my province pregnant with
power, unilingual, suffering the alienation of her half-
brothers and half-sisters of the West.

First Mate:
Suffer the children...

Justice of the Piece:

I saw what might have been, what is, what will be,
periodically cry out with abduction & murder. I saw
the battle on the Plains of Abraham like I would a
balloon...

First Mate:

I saw a hundred thousand march to war on a cloudy
day in December, 25 below.

Justice of the Piece:

I saw the battle.

First Mate:

I saw below the city unfurl its Registered Retirement
Savings Plan, burrowing its way into the infinite land
of 15 billion dollar programs to build an industrial
complex at Al Subdil in the eastern province of Saudi
Arabia. There goes another eastern province.

Justice of the Piece:

I saw my sleepwalking country in a half-way house
on Bleury with a guitar case and camera.

First Mate:

I saw foreign investment and more foreign investment
and more more foreign investment settle on the
shores of the St Lawrence like so many ants
on a heap of rotten eggs.

Justice of the Piece:

I saw my sleeping country wake from its deep mediocrity only to discover a malignant tomorrow in its left breast. I saw my sleepwalking country with a guitar case lying open on the sidewalk on a Saturday afternoon in July. I threw him a loon to hear him sing of California and the beaches and the girls with blonde hair and love.

First Mate:

He'll cut his hair next week, move back to Ottawa, think Kaybeck is Kweebeck and opt for Spanish as a second language.

Justice of the Piece:

O Can a dance without partners exist?

First Mate:

Merry go round the mountain, merry go round the sky.

Justice of the Piece:

I saw the flags waving, I couldn't help it, I saw the army marching. I couldn't mistake it, I saw their swords gleaming bright in the sunlight, I didn't restrain it, moving with ease and grace through the crowded streets of my city. I saw their lips moving with unmistakable joual, I couldn't dig it. I saw the army marching into the town, I couldn't believe it.

I couldn't stop seeing the merciless hand of fate
pronounce them country and wife, man and strife, till
death do your part.

First Mate:

Semen.

II

Justice of the Piece:
Come, let us make or break a nation.

First Mate:
Aren't English and French just made for each other?

Justice of the Piece:
Made for washing each other.

First Mate:
Made for watching each other washing each other.

Justice of the Piece:
I can make out a pair of eyes. What do you make of
it?

First Mate:
I make it a wrong turn heading down Sherbrooke,
going West.

Justice of the Piece:
Make yourself comfortable, make room baby, make room all around, for a change is being made, a change is being made all around, change is being made in nickels and dimes. What do you make of it?

First Mate:
I make it a duet, francophones dancing in the streets of Ontario, Grand, de la Savane, Peel, Fleet, Hochelaga, Galt, Aylmer, Remembrance.

Justice of the Piece:
Make yourself believe a change is being made, make a change by believing a change is being made, make change happen, one for all—all arms and legs. What do you make of it?

First Mate:
I make it a maple leaf & fleur de lys as naked lovers embracing. I heard someone say, in simultaneous translation, "Love Conquers All" or was it just the daily shifting of earwax...

Justice of the Piece:
There is emotion excited by novel unexpected things: there is astonishment mixed with perplexity, curiosity, and there in the second row, yes, admiration. I should not be surprised.

First Mate:
Faisons-le avec Mary. Faisons-le avec Janey et Mary. Faisons-le avec Mary et Merle et Jacques et Patricia et Marcel et Jennifer et René. Faisons le bien.

Justice of the Piece:
What do you make of the act of interfering unlawfully in a suit by helping either party by giving money etc. to carry it on? What do you make of it? Let's make a rule.

First Mate:
Pack your suitcase and head for Toronto. How do you make a fortune?

Justice of the Piece:
Make a fortune by making war. Make war against the disease of language and culture that threatens our suburbs by infiltrating its hideous thoughts thru TV antennas—now only $99.99!

First Mate:
You can make the team by swallowing goldfish followed by an infinitive. If you watch your watch you can make the train behave.

Justice of the Piece:
Make the train behave by making 500 miles the next day and so on.

First Mate:
So on the train make the goldfish behave.

Justice of the Piece:
By following them with an imperative.

First Mate:
Let's make it with Janey. Let's make it with Janey and Mary.

Justice of the Piece:
Let's make it good. Make an oath.

First Mate:
Maudit parapluie, if it ever stops raining out here I'm gonna stomp those Mae Wests in the gutter. I swear maudit tabarnacle shit I swear by the power invested in this paradise on becoming a disabled veteran out of the force of good fuck I swear Big John...

Justice of the Piece:
If we ever get outa this alive we'll have the sheriff's head and then some too. What do you make of it?

First Mate:
Make merry friends, for today I shall pass and who knows what tomorrow may bring in the mail. What do you make of it?

Justice of the Piece:
The white paper has become the blueprint we will never forget. War we will never forget. War we will never regret.

First Mate:
If this is the second movement, like first, second, third, fourth, why can't we just say so? I mean, war we will never forget, a wart we will never forget.

Justice of the Piece:
Make merry, my friends, make haste, mes amis, for the hour is struck in our land; the crickets' chirp is stopped, the machine is gone full TILT. What do you make of it?

First Mate:
It's a Bell Canada bill made out to monsieur, a little love note from the tele-boutique, I just can't understand it.

Justice of the Piece:
Make believe this is all not happening, not here, not now, not ever, not in any way possible, not to you, not to me, not to him, not to her, whether we like it or not. What do you make of it?

First Mate:
A frog fable, to be sure. One day I meet this frog in
the elevator, first second third fourth fifth on the sixth
seventh eighth on the ninth of December, I think it
was.

III

Justice of the Piece:
French schools or English schools...

First Mate:
School English schoolchildren in French schools...

Justice of the Piece:
School French schoolchildren in English schools...

First Mate:
School French schoolchildren in French schools...

Justice of the Piece:
School immigrant schoolchildren in French schools...

First Mate:
School the children of immigrant schoolchildren
schooled in French schools or English schools in
French schools...

Justice of the Piece:

School the nieces of immigrant schoolchildren in
English schools and nephews of immigrant school-
children in French schools.

First Mate:

School the famous children of immigrant school-
children in French schools...

Justice of the Piece:

School children of immigrant schoolchildren in the
ways to make them vote for French schools for
English schoolchildren or children of immigrant
schoolchildren, disestablishmentarianism,
socialization, despotism, fear of science and
unidentified material phenomena, boxing games.

First Mate:

I can't get over it!

The Language Cops

Une

We are the language cops
We are the real Québécois
We stand on guard for thee
Our dossier full with les language laws. Oui!
Our deeds, chez-nous, when
We purify ensemble
Are pure laine québécoise
As natural gas après les beans
Or Arrêts without Stops
On every sainted street.

Words without accents, words with apostrophes,
Dangerous words we battle constantly.

Those who first hauled them
With Bill 101, to language jails,
We remember them as Saints Unique
Visionaries, gens du pays,
As the language cops
The real Québécois.

Deux

Sign crimes we see everywhere
In l'état du Québec.
These do appear:
See there, là,
"Hamburger" on a greasy menu
Là, a "Dunkin" on a box
And voices are
On French radio, singing
More Madonna and more Vanilla
Than René Simard.

Let us be vigilant
In l'état du Québec.
Let us also guard
Such québécois monuments as
Le Harvey's, Le Canadian Tire, Le Miniput
On boulevard René-Lévesque
Behaving as good citoyens
OK hostie—

Not like les autres
In les suburbs là

Trois

This is the West Island.
This is anglo land.
Here, là,
Les For Sale signs are raised.
Here they contemplate
The low offers on their estates and
Under their breath mutter "maudit tabernacle."

C'est comme ça
In Tête Carré land.
They sit alone
At the hour when we chez nous
Tremble with Les Filles de Caleb.
Their lips that should speak French
Sip English bloody Breakfast Tea.

Quatre

The signs are there:
There are signs everywhere
In this land of the Other Language
In their restaurants specialising
In dry roast beef and Baby Duck.
Mon Dieu!
A crime against our palate as well as our laws.

46

In this last of Bloke places
We hunt ensemble
And take down their names and
Signs that are outside
And are bigger than ours.

Signless, unless
The signs reappear
As le vrai de vrai
Only fleur-de-lys blue
Of l'état du Québec
Le grand prix
Of the language cops.

Cinq

Language cops, Language cops
Do not sleep, do not sleep
English signs are all around you
English signs are all around you
Take them down
Take them down

Between the apostrophe
And the circonflexe
Between the present
And the plus-que-parfait
Fall our Shadows

A Sign for our Québec

Between Allo Police
And The Gazette
Between Passe Partout
And Mr Dress Up
Fall our Shadows

Vivre Service Libre

Between le poutine
And le smoked meat
Entre boulevard René-Lévesque est
And Dorchester Boulevard West
Between nous
And them
Fall our Shadows

A Sign for our Québec

For Victory is Ours.
Vive Le & Vive La!
Sens unique is the way.

This is the way our battle ends.
Il fini comme ça. To the victor the spoils:
We winter in Miami, summer in Maine,
Dollar at par, in which language, who the hell cares.

Au Canada!

Canada we've given it all away
and now we're nothing.
Canada $00.86US December 1990.
We can't understand our own languages.
Canada when will we end this maudit guerre?
Mange la merde! All dressed!
I don't feel good, lâche pas la patate!
Canada when will we be a mosaic?
When will we take off our winter tires?
When will we look at ourselves on CBC?
When will we be worthy of our Native Canadians?
Canada why are our libraries full
of American bestsellers?
Canada when will we teach CanLit to our MPs?
I'm sick of our Royal commissions.
When can we go to any province and feel at home?
Canada, after all, it's moi et toi
qui sont perfectly bilingue.
Eh/n'est ce pas?
Our selling out is too much for me.
Who wants to be Canadian? To be or not to be?
There must be some other way to settle this debate.

Mulroney is in the States.
I know he's on their payroll.
Are you becoming the 51st state
or is this a Free Trade joke?

I'm trying to come to a consensus.
I refuse to give up my Canajunism.
Canada Stop/Arrête. I know que je fais hostie!
Canada the acid snowflakes are falling.
I won't read the Globe & Mail, just Croc.
Every day somebody goes on to become a senator.
Canada I feel sentimental about Pierre Trudeau.

I don' t know the words to the national anthem.
Canada I used to be an immigrant when I was a kid
now I'm an allophone.
I have bilingual visions and multicultural vibrations.
I dance ethnic dances every chance I get.
You should see me reading Canadian poetry.
I am talking to myself again.
My friends think I'm perfectly crazy.
My mind is made up for me.
There is going to be a referendum.
Canada I still haven't told you what you did
to la plume de ma tante
...after class

Are we going to let our cultural life be run by
ABC/NBC/CBS/PBS?
We're obsessed with ABC/NBC/CBS/PBS.
We watch them all day
Their logos stare at us whenever we channel hop.
We sit in our homes for days and watch
As The Stomach Turns, Arsenio Hole,
The Price is Wrong, and The Grossout Whorero shows.

50

Hungry America likes to eat out.
Wants to make us into Ronald MacPoutines.
Wants to take the musical ride out of our Mounties.
Needs Canadian Time & Life.
Wants our auto plants shut down
Wants us to see the USA in our Japanese Chevrolets.
Wants us to fill up at Uncle Sam's,
wear its L.L. Beans, buy at its factory outlets,
smoke its Camels, and drink
its Real Thing 24 hours a day.

They're always selling us the American Dream.
Canadians are serious about the American Dream.
Canadians are serious.
Everybody is serious but me.

Au Canada
how can I write my litany
in your maudit sell out mood?
Canada Front Page Challenge must not die.
Canada we are the Dionne Quintuplets.
Canada when I was six poppa took me to the Forum
and the game was good
and everybody was a Canadiens fan.
It was all so magnifique.
Je me souviens, I remember
how good the team was in 1976.
Guy Lafleur was in bloom.
Every year was a Stanley Cup.

Oka is rising against us.
We haven't got a Loto of a chance.
We'd better consider our national resources.
Our national resources consist of
two official languages,
billions of debts,
a not-withstanding clause
Ben Johnson on steroids
and millions on the dole.

I say nothing about the too few rich
Who are GSTing us to death.
whose money hides in tax shelters abroad
in numbered accounts under lock and key.
Who are abolishing health care programs.
The education, she is next to go.

Help.
Canada this is serious.
Canada is this you I see on Newsworld?
My ambition is to be Canadian
whatever that means.

Canada you don't really believe
that there is such a thing as Free Trade.
It's like Free Lunch.
Comme Libre Service and Free Ride.
It's like Free Speech.
Canada trade Mulroney!

We don't believe our officials' comments anymore.
We're too farsighted.
We have seen the future and it is
Canucks.

Au Canada, ça suffit!
OK! Allons-y, hostie!
OK! Let us go, you and I!
Let us turn our backs on this,
Let us put on our mukluks and our tuques
Let us mount our skidoos and ride proudly
into the glowing Northern Lights.

The Only Canadian In Bangor, Maine
Turns His Thoughts Homeward

Come my Two Solitudes,
let us save Canada Bonds
let us find our serious identity
let us dump maple syrup on the White House
let us make the English speak English
       in Québec & French everywhere else
let us torture our senators
       by making them stay awake,
let us purge the Bloc Québécois
let us encourage our natives
       to emigrate
       so we can build James Bay III, IV, V
let us make the CBC abandon news
       and documentaries
let us entice Florida to separate
       and become our eleventh province
let us destroy tourism
by having road signs that mean nothing,
let us trade Newfoundland for St Pierre et Miquelon
let us sell our politicans
       to Latin America
(Is it true that one of our national leaders
       is intelligent?)
let us capture and terrorize Detroit,
let us unite
       French and English in debt,

let us do it on skidoos,
let us have ten Prime Ministers
        at the same time,
let us have no official languages,
let us give Canada Council grants
        to the most ignorant MP
let us determine who that might be
let us teach joual in Westmount
let us threaten to join the USA
        and at the last moment do it,

My two solitudes come,
our sovereignty is waiting for us somewhere
north of Sault Ste Marie
south of St Louis de Ha-Ha
let us find it quickly
let us stand on guard
for another year or two,
or until someone makes us a better offer.

Printed by
Ateliers Graphiques Marc Veilleux Inc.
Cap-Saint-Ignace Qué.
in December 1991